Savory Mug Cooking

Deb Graham

Savory Mug Cooking

Deb Graham

Other Books By Deb Graham:

Tips From The Cruise Addict's Wife

Hungry Kids Camp Fire Cookbook

Quick and Clever Kids' Crafts

Awesome Science Experiments for Kids

It's great to cook for large family or group of friends, but sometimes it's just you, and you're hungry. What's better than a warm meal in a cozy mug?

You know there are lots of Make-A-Cake-In-A-Mug recipes out there, but what about when you want a real meal, not just something sweet? Here are recipes for quiche, omelets, soups, dips and spreads, even meatballs, and jerk chicken! All are single-serving, made of fresh ingredients---no mixes here!

Every recipe can be made in under 4 minutes, right in your own mug. Perfect for those mornings when you're running late, or want a hot fresh lunch at the office. They're also great for after-school snacks; mouth-watering, delicious, nutritious, and so simple a child can make them!

Why should you try mug cooking?

Tips to Make Mug Cooking Even Easier:

Snacks In A Mug

   Nachos In A Mug

   Pretzel Dip

   Peanut Pretzel Wands

   Peanut-Free Pretzel Wands

   Fruit Dip

   Layered Bean Dip In A Mug

   Melted Cheese Spread

   Pizza Spread

Breakfast In A Mug

   Basic Scrambled Eggs And Cheese In A Mug

   Sausage and Eggs Breakfast

   French Toast in a Mug

   Stuffed French Toast (variation)

   Denver Omelet In A Mug

   Bacon Omelet In A Mug

   Quiche In A Mug

   Pizza Egg Breakfast In A Mug

   Blueberry Oatmeal In A Mug

   "Baked" Oatmeal

   Apples And Oatmeal In A Mug

   Banana Oatmeal In A Mug

Green Eggs And Ham In A Mug

Lunch or Dinner In A Mug

Greek Lemon Soup

Tuna Sandwich Spread

Baked Beans in a Mug

Potato Soup Mix in a Mug

Variation: Instant Cheesy Soup In A Mug

Chicken and Rice Casserole in a Mug

Easy Microwave Chicken and Beans In A Mug

Macaroni And Cheese In A Mug

Jerk Chicken Wings

Chicken and Peppers

Meatballs and Sauce

Very Garlic Shrimp

Beans and Wieners In A Mug

Meatloaf in a Mug

Vegetables And Fruits In A Mug

Corn On The Cob

Asparagus

Garlicky Broccoli

Italian Zucchini

Baked Apple

Apples with Raisins

Peaches and Cream

Chunky Applesauce In A Mug

Warm Beverages In A Mug

   Honey Milk Punch

   Vanilla Steamer

   Hot Lemonade

   Ginger Tea

   Wassail

   Hot Spiced Milk

A Couple Of Sweets In A Mug

   S'Mores Goo

   Krispie Rice Treat For One

   Very Nearly Thin Mints

   Banana Dessert

The End (?) and a Plea:

Why should you try mug cooking?

First, it's fun! Making a whole meal in a mug in minutes can't be beat.

It's versatile! It's portable! Your favorite mug even has a handle to grab on the run.

It's creative! Once you see how easy mug cooking is, you'll be hooked. Soon you'll be on the look out for other meals you can convert to mug-size meals.

It's just the right size! Mug meals are single servings; you might be tempted by a whole platter of leftovers, but these are just enough for one.

It's wholesome! All are made of fresh ingredients; no commercial mixes made of stuff you can't pronounce.

It's easy! Each recipe has minimal prep---you could easily place a bowl, spoon, and you favorite mug in your desk at work, bring pre-chopped ingredients form home, and make a hot meal in the break room microwave in a couple of minutes. You'd be back at your desk, sipping your hot lunch before the fast-food place finishes taking the order.

It's made just the way you like it! Feel free to vary according to preference; leave out the cheese, add more bacon, stir in fresh herbs; it's *your* lunch!

Clean up is quick and easy, and makes no wrappers to trash or pots to wash. Clean your mug, and off you go. You didn't even dirty a plate!

It's inexpensive! You already own a mug and a microwave, and there are ingredients in your refrigerator. Face it...lunch at the corner shop adds up quick.

Tips to Make Mug Cooking Even Easier:

I recommend buttering or using cooking spray on the inside of every mug; it makes clean up faster. If you do get a stuck-on spot, simply soak the mug, and get back to it later!

Speaking of clean up... some of these recipes produce quite a bit of steam inside the microwave. Use it to your advantage! Remove the mug after cooking, and while it's standing, simple swipe out the microwave's inside with a rag. The steam loosens any prior stuck-on messes, and your food will be ready to eat before you've thrown the rag away! Maybe I'm lazy. Or efficient.

What kind of mug should you use? Just your standard ceramic mug! Be sure it's microwave safe, with no metal trim. Arcing is cool, but it ruins both your microwave and your lunch.

What size mug are we talking here? Up to you, within reason! Smaller mugs allow the batter or food to poof up over top, but could overflow. Larger ones let you dig down into the mug. Either way! 12 oz is a fine middle ground.

For recipes that will puff up, like eggs, fill mugs about half way or three-quarters full. If it's going to boil, like Meatballs and Sauce, leave about 1 1/2 inches at the top.

Covering your meal as it cooks prevents splatters. I use cheap paper coffee filters; just keep a stack on the microwave. Waxed paper also makes a fine cover. I avoid plastic wrap. Yes, I know it's safe, but I don't believe that. The idea of melted plastic in my lunch gives me heebie-jeebies. It's another reason I cook my own food, instead of those plastic-packed freezer meals!

These recipes are made in a standard microwave. Be aware that times vary, depending on the microwave's power. Undercook your recipe, then add a few more seconds if needed. Generally, cook until the food looks nearly done: eggs almost set, batter no longer shiny, vegetables crisp-tender. By the time it stands for a minute, it'll be perfect.

As with all microwave cooking, let the food stand a minute or two to settle after cooking. Microwaved food is hotter than Death Valley when it first comes out. Let it rest! You'll be less likely to burn your mouth, and the cooking is more even. Keep a potholder nearby, too. This is lunch, not a first aid class.

All the recipes here are single serving. If you have more than one person, or want a baked apple with your soup, feel free to make more mugs! Just add to the cooking time.

If you're cooking more than one mug, arrange them in a circle, not crowded in the center of the microwave.

Egg yolk explosions can be dramatic, and a chore to clean up. To avoid a loud mess, be sure to thoroughly mix the eggs in any recipe before cooking.

Not all of these recipes are precise. They are more *method* than exact recipes. My style of cooking has been described as Loosey-Goosey--- I put together what sounds good together, and cook it until it's done. I recommend trying the recipes as written once, then get creative next time!

Get your mug, let's cook!

Snacks in a Mug

Ahh, your stomach has an empty corner, or you need a mid-day munch.

These snacks are good any time of the day!

Nachos in a Mug

Add some leftover cooked meat, and it's a fine lunch!

Spray a mug with cooking spray. Fill 3 /4 full of corn chips. Sprinkle with shredded cheddar cheese. Heat 20 seconds, until cheese is melted. Drizzle with salsa. *Next time, add avocado, olives, scallions...*

Pretzel Dip in a Mug

Microwave 1 /4 cup peanut butter with 1/ 4 chocolate chips, either dark or milk variety. Stir until smooth. Dip pretzel sticks and munch away.

Peanut Pretzel Wands in a Mug

Melt 1 /4 cup chocolate chips with 2 T peanut butter in mug, about 30 seconds. Stir. Dip both ends of pretzel rod into mixture, then roll in crushed peanuts

Peanut-Free Pretzel Wands in a Mug

Warm chocolate-hazelnut spread (like Nutella) in a mug. Dip both ends of pretzel rods into the goo, then roll in crunchy dry cereal.

Fruit Dip in a Mug

3 oz cream cheese (low fat is fine) and 2 T brown sugar. Heat about 30 seconds, until bubbly. Dip fresh fruit in it. Berries, melons, and apples are especially nice.

Layered Bean Dip In A Mug

Add leftover taco meat or shredded chicken to make this a filling main dish.

Spray mug with cooking spray. Stir together 1/2 mug of canned drained black beans, or refried beans with 2-3 T salsa. Cover with coffee filter or paper. Heat through. Top with chopped olives, avocado, shredded cheese, more salsa, a blop of sour cream. Scoop with corn chips.

Melted Cheese Spread in a Mug

Deceptively easy, deceptively delicious

Stir together 1/ 4 cup mayonnaise, and 3 oz shredded Swiss cheese. Microwave 1 minute. Stir in 2 scallions, minced. Spread on crackers or pita triangles.

Pizza Spread in a Mug

Oh, yum!

Melt handful of grated mozzarella cheese with 3-4 T bottled pasta sauce, any variety. Stir in minced pepperoni slices, chopped olives, and minced fresh basil. Spread on pita chips

Breakfast In A Mug

Filling, warm breakfast, faster than a drive through!

Basic Scrambled Eggs And Cheese in a Mug

Cheddar cheese is fine, but experiment with other types next time.

Spray mug with cooking spray. Stir together 2 eggs and 1 T milk, with salt and pepper to taste, in your mug. Microwave 45 seconds, stir, and repeat until egg is nearly set. Sprinkle with grated cheese.

Sausage and Eggs Breakfast in a Mug

Break apart frozen hash brown potatoes, any variety. Cook with 3 links sausage, crumbled, until no longer pink, in your mug. Drain. Stir in 2 eggs and bell pepper bits, taking care to break yolks. Microwave until eggs are almost set, stirring once. Even better with grated cheese on top.

French Toast in a Mug

Tastes like a warm bread pudding. Vary the bread; a bagel, French bread...

Break up 1 slice any type bread into buttered mug. Combine 1 egg and 3 T milk, and pour over bread. Drizzle with 1 tsp melted butter. You can also add a drop of vanilla extract and a sprinkle of cinnamon. Microwave 1- 2 minutes, until egg is no longer runny. Serve with syrup or jelly.

Stuffed French Toast (variation)

Like a sweet cheesecake---for breakfast!

Same as above, except spread bread with thin layer of cream cheese and strawberry jam before breaking into mug.

Denver Omelet in a Mug

Spray mug with cooking spray. Stir together 2 eggs and 1 T milk, with salt and pepper to taste, in the mug. Microwave 15 seconds, stir, and add in add in 1 T diced bell pepper (any color), and 2 T chopped cooked ham. Cook until egg is nearly set. Sprinkle with grated cheese.

Bacon Omelet in a Mug

Wrap 2 slices bacon in several layers of white paper towels. Microwave 1 minute. Discard paper, and chop bacon.   Mix with 2 eggs in your mug, and microwave 1 minute. Stir. Continue cooking until egg is nearly set. Sprinkle with grated cheddar or Colby cheese.

Quiche in a Mug

Variations: add spinach, cooked bacon, Gruyere cheese, herbs, etc

Tear 1 /4 bagel or similar amount of French bread into fingernail sized cubes in a buttered mug. Mix 1 egg with 2 T milk, salt and pepper. Pour over bread. Drop in 2 teaspoons cream cheese, and 1/2 slice cooked ham, diced. Microwave about 1 minute ten seconds. Sprinkle on fresh parsley or chives.

Pizza Egg Breakfast in a Mug

Stir 2 tbsp. canned crushed tomatoes and a sprinkle of Italian seasoning in a bowl. Set aside. Spray mug with cooking spray. Combine 2 eggs, 1 oz shredded mozzarella or jack cheese, and 6 slices pepperoni in a mug. Cook 1 minute. Stir. Microwave additional 30 seconds. Stir in tomatoes, and cook another 20 seconds, until egg is set.

Blueberry Oatmeal in a Mug

This makes wonderful, warm, dense oatmeal. Even better with milk on top

In a greased mug, combine 1/4 cup regular oats, 1 t brown sugar, 1/4 cup blueberries, 1 egg, 2 T milk, and a dash of cinnamon. Cook 2 minutes, stirring after one minute. Let stand 1 minute.

"Baked" Oatmeal in a Mug

Delicious on its own. Topped with yogurt, it's pretty perfect.

Melt 1 T butter in your mug. Swirl to coat inside. Stir in 1 1/2 T brown sugar, 1 egg, 1/8 teaspoon cinnamon, and 1 T milk. Stir in 1 / 2 cup quick-cooking oats, stirring to moisten. Add in 1 T dried fruits, any variety (cranberries, raisins, apricots, etc.) Microwave 1 1/ 2 minutes. The oatmeal will pull away from the sides of the mug when it's done.

Apples And Oatmeal in a Mug

Stir in a mug: 1/2 cup dry oats, 1/2 cup milk (any variety), 1 egg,   1 /2 apple, diced, 1/4 tsp cinnamon and 1 T honey. Microwave 1 1/ 2 minutes.

Banana Oatmeal in a Mug

Mash 1/ 2 of a banana in a mug with a fork. Mix with 1 /2 cup quick oats, 1 egg, 1 /2 cup milk, 2 T sugar. Cook about 2 minutes, until set. Let stand 1 minute.

Green Eggs And Ham in a Mug

Spray mug with cooking spray. Microwave 1 handful chopped spinach leaves in a mug until wilted, about 30 seconds. Blot liquid with a paper towel. Beat 2 eggs, and mix with spinach. Microwave 1 minute. Stir in 2 sliced cooked ham, chopped, and 1 scallion, chopped. Cook one minute, until egg is just set. Sprinkle on grated white cheese.

Lunch or Dinner in a Mug

Anybody can make a muffin in a cup, but YOU can make a meal!

Greek Lemon Soup in a Mug

Fill mug 2/ 3 full of chicken broth. Stir in 3 T instant rice and a sprinkle of black pepper. Microwave until boiling. Let stand, while you stir together 2 eggs, with 2 T lemon juice. Stir egg mixture in to hot soup, and cook additional 25 seconds. Garnish with chopped parsley.

Tuna Sandwich Spread in a Mug

You could mix up the tuna spread at home, and warm it at lunchtime.

Combine in a large mug: can of tuna, drained, 1 T mayonnaise, 2 T pickle relish, and 1 oz shredded cheese (jack, mozzarella, cheddar, or Colby). Heat until bubbly. Spread on toast or baguette. *Next time, jazz up the spread with grated carrot, diced celery or peppers, or whatever else appeals to you.*

Baked Beans in a Mug

Stir together: 1 T brown sugar, 2 strips cooked bacon,* 1 tsp minced onion, 1 /2 tsp mustard. Add enough canned pork and beans to fill mug 3 /4 full. Stir to combine. Microwave, covered, 2-3 minutes, stirring twice.

Wrap 2 slices bacon in several layers of white paper towels. Microwave 1 minute. Discard paper; it's better that way.

Potato Soup Mix in a Mug

Tastes even better with grated cheddar cheese on top

Stir together: 1 /3 cup instant mashed potatoes, 2 T dry milk, 2 chicken bouillon cubes (crushed), 2 t minced onion (dried is fine), spring of parsley, chopped, or 1 t dry parsley, dash salt and pepper, or seasoning salt. Fill mug with water, leaving an inch at top. Microwave 2 minutes, stirring in the middle. Let stand 2 minutes.

Variation: Instant Cheesy Soup in a Mug

Make Potato Soup Mix in a Mug as directed, except stir in 2 T grated parmesan cheese before serving. *Another variation: add in chopped cooked bacon.*

Chicken and Rice Casserole in a Mug

Leftover cooked chicken from dinner? Bring it along!

In a big mug, combine 1/3 cup instant rice, dash celery salt, 1 t dried onion flakes, 1 t dried parsley flakes, 1/2 cup water, 1 T butter, 1 can chunk chicken (drained), 2 T shredded cheddar cheese. Microwave 2-3 minutes. Stir twice while cooking. Let stand 4 minutes.

Easy Microwave Chicken and Beans in a Mug

This can be enjoyed on flour tortillas, baguette, or just gobbled up with your fork

Cook 1/ 2 cup fresh spinach in a mug until melted. Blot liquid with a paper towel. Stir in 1 /3 cup canned black beans (drained) and a handful of cooked chicken (leftovers are ideal) with 3 T salsa. Heat until bubbly. Stir, and add in 1 /4 cup shredded cheddar cheese.

Macaroni and Cheese in a Mug

Tastes much better than the boxed stuff, and it's faster, too! Experiment with your favorite cheeses, and add in a few shrimp or mushrooms if desired. Place mug on a (paper) plate, because the water often overflows the mug as it boils.

Fill a mug with 1 /2 cup water and 1/3 cup dry pasta. Any shape is fine, just be sure it fits under the water's surface. Microwave total of 4 minutes, stirring at intervals. If pasta is still too firm, add 1 T water and cook one more minute. Add in 1 /4 cup milk and 1 /2 cup shredded cheese, any variety. Heat 30 seconds more. Stir to combine.

Jerk Chicken Wings in a Mug

Toss 4-6 split chicken wings, 2 t vegetable oil, and 3 tablespoons jerk seasoning in a bowl. Arrange in large mug. Cover loosely, and cook until meat is no longer pink, about 3 minutes.

Chicken and Peppers in a Mug

Minute Rice makes a nice brown rice that's a breeze to make in a mug! Cook it separately, in a second mug, then combine on your plate.

Chop meat from one chicken drumstick. Cook in a mug, covered, 1 minute. Add in half bell pepper, sliced, 1/ 2 tsp soy sauce, and dash garlic powder. Cook until meat is no longer pink, about 2 minutes. Serve over rice.

Meatballs and Sauce in a Mug

See Macaroni and Cheese recipe for easy pasta cooking method. It's easy to make the meatballs at home, then cook on the go. You could substitute bottled pasta sauce if you prefer---it's your lunch!

Mix 4 oz bulk Italian sausage with 1 slice bread, torn into cubes. Form into 2 meatballs. Place in buttered mug, cover, and microwave 1 minute, until no longer pink in the middle. Drain liquid. Pour over some crushed tomatoes, and sprinkle with garlic powder and oregano to taste. Cook another minute. Serve over toasted bread, or with noodles.

Very Garlic Shrimp in a Mug

Pass the napkins!

Place 4-5 large unpeeled shrimp in a mug. Add in 1 T butter, 1 clove garlic, smashed, dash of lemon juice, and a small pinch of red pepper flakes. Cover loosely and cook until shrimp is just pink. Let stand 2 minutes.

Beans and Wieners in a Mug

Cut a hot dog or smokie sausage into slices. Fill mug half full with canned pork and beans, and stir in hot dog. Cover and microwave 90 seconds. Serve with toast or bread.

Meatloaf in a Mug

Combine 1/4 lb ground beef (or ground pork or ground chicken), 1 tsp onion soup mix, 2 T milk, 2 T dry oats, 1 T ketchup. Pat into greased mug, leaving a trough at one side to catch grease. Cover and cook 3 minutes, or until inside shows no pink. Drain. Spread more ketchup on top if desired.

Vegetables and Fruits in a Mug

Corn On The Cob in a Mug

Shuck and de-hair a cob of corn. Wrap in a white paper towel, and wet the towel. Stand in a mug, and cook 2-3 minutes. Serve with butter, salt, parmesan cheese, chili powder, bacon bits, or soy sauce.

Asparagus in a Mug

Arrange 4-6 asparagus stalks in mug, standing up, with 1 T water in the bottom of the mug. Loosely tent with waxed paper. Microwave 2-4 minutes, just until crisp-tender. Sprinkle with lemon pepper.

Garlicky Broccoli in a Mug

Toss chopped broccoli tops with melted butter, a sprinkle of water, garlic bits, lemon pepper, and dash of salt. Arrange loosely in mug. Cover, and cook until crisp-tender, about 2 minutes.

Italian Zucchini in a Mug

Even better with parmesan cheese on top!

Slice half of a small zucchini, and dice one tomato. Toss in bowl with smashed garlic clove, 1 t olive oil, fresh basil, and salt and pepper. Cover and cook about 2 minutes. Let stand.

Baked Apple in a Mug

Cut and core an apple. Place in mug, and sprinkle with a few cinnamon red-hot candies, or more than a few if you like spicy apples. Cover and cook until tender, about 3 minutes.

Apples with Raisins in a Mug

Core and cube an apple, and place in a mug. Sprinkle with 2 T brown sugar, a thin slice of butter, 1/ 4 tsp cinnamon, and some raisins. Microwave until tender.

Peaches and Cream in a Mug

Cut a ripe peach in half, and remove pit. Place 1 t
brown sugar and thin slice butter with dash of
cinnamon in the cavity. Reassemble peach, and
place in mug. Cook 2 minutes, until soft. Serve with
sour cream or whipped cream.

Chunky Applesauce in a Mug

Peel, core, and dice an apple into a mug. Sprinkle
with 1 T sugar and dash cinnamon. Add 1 tsp water.
Cover and microwave 2 minutes. Stir.

Warm Beverages in a Mug

What's nicer than a warm mug in your hands on a chilly day?

Honey Milk Punch in a Mug

Fill mug with milk and stir in 1 T honey, and a drop of vanilla. Heat, and sprinkle with freshly grated nutmeg.

Vanilla Steamer in a Mug

Fill your mug with milk, any type. Stir in 2 tsp sugar, and dash of cinnamon. Heat until warm. Add in 1 tsp vanilla extract. Even nicer with whipped cream.

Hot Lemonade in a Mug

Squeeze half of a lemon into mug. Throw in peel for extra flavor. Add 2 tsp honey or sugar. Fill mug with water, heat until steaming. Remove peel before serving.

Ginger Tea in a Mug

Place 4-6 thin slices raw ginger (no need to peel) in a mug with 2 T lime or lemon juice. Fill with water. Heat to nearly boiling. Let steep 4-5 minutes, remove ginger slices and serve.

Wassail in a Mug

Try it with pineapple, or cranberry juices

Fill mug 3/ 4 full of orange juice. Add 2 whole clove, or a light sprinkle of ground cloves, and 1 orange slice. Add a sprinkle of cinnamon, or stir with whole cinnamon stick. Heat until steaming.

Hot Spiced Milk in a Mug

Place in your favorite mug: dash each cinnamon, ground ginger, ground cloves, and scant dash ground nutmeg. Add 1/ 4 tsp vanilla, and 4 tsp sugar. Float a strip of orange peel for extra flavor (optional). Fill mug with milk, and heat to steaming. Stir to dissolve sugar.

A Couple Of Sweets In A Mug

Yes, a virtuous lunch is a great thing, but sometimes you have a nagging sweet tooth

S'Mores Goo in a Mug

In a mug, melt 5 Hershey's kisses (or 4 T chocolate chips) with 2 marshmallows. Stir to partially blend. Sprinkle on 1 crushed graham cracker. Eat while warm.

Krispie Rice Treat For One in a Mug

Yay---no reason to share, and no reason to eat the whole pan, either!

Melt 5 marshmallows with 1 t butter and dash of vanilla (optional) in your mug, just until puffy. Watch it-- it takes under 10 seconds for marshmallows to puff! Stir in handful of krispie

rice cereal. Eat with a spoon, or let cool long
enough to pop out of the mug.

Very Nearly Thin Mints in a Mug

Melt 1 /2 mug dark chocolate chips. Stir until smooth. Stir in few drops peppermint oil. While warm, spread on buttery-round crackers (Ritz type). Reheat if it gets thick.

Banana Dessert in a Mug

Peel and slice a banana into a mug. Sprinkle a few mini marshmallows, and a handful of chocolate chips. Heat until warmed through. *Variation:* try peanut butter chips, shredded, coconut, drained bottled cherries, and whatever else sounds good next time.

The End (?) and a Plea:

Are you a fan of Savory Mug Cooking? I knew you'd enjoy it!

Be sure to read my other books:

Hungry Kids Campfire Cookbook

Quick and Clever Kids' Crafts

Awesome Science Experiments for Kids

AND DON'T MISS

Tips From The Cruise Addict's Wife

If you've ever even considered a cruise vacation, you'd enjoy _**Tips From The Cruise Addict's Wife**_. Besides being crammed with more tips and hints than you'll find anywhere else, including how to save money, and plan a great vacation, it's loaded with funny stories that will have you laughing aloud as you read them to whoever is near.

Please take time to leave a five-star review of this book. It'll take you under three minutes, and can be anonymous if you'd prefer. I greatly appreciate it!

Thanks!

Made in the USA
San Bernardino, CA
30 December 2015